Bug Alert!

by Bruce Parker
Illustrated by Bill Ledger

OXFORD
UNIVERSITY PRESS

In this story ...

Ben
(Sprint)

Ben is super fast! He can run faster than a racing car. Once, he ran five times round the school grounds in under ten seconds.

Magnus
(caretaker)

Mrs Molten
(teacher)

Ben was late. The bell was going to ring any second, and he was nowhere near Mrs Molten's classroom.

Ben raced up the stairs, along the corridor, through the classroom door, and then *THUMP!* He ran straight into somebody and fell backwards.

Ben leaped up. "Sorry," he said. Then his mouth fell open. He couldn't believe it! He'd crashed straight into a school inspector – a *super*intendent.

"Well," the superintendent snapped, "this is not a good start."

Ben had forgotten that there was a school inspection today. If only he hadn't been late!

"Mrs Molten," the superintendent said crossly, "I need a cup of tea to calm my nerves."

"Of course," said Mrs Molten. She asked another pupil to show the superintendent to the staffroom.

As she left, the superintendent gave Mrs Molten a stern look. "I hope the staffroom is clean. Dirt attracts rats, mice, cockroaches …"

The superintendent shuddered. "If I have any reason to think this school is not clean, I shall close it down at once!"

Mrs Molten looked unhappy. "Our school is very clean, Superintendent."

The superintendent glared at Mrs Molten. "I shall be back soon to observe your lesson," she said coldly. Then she marched out of the room.

The class settled down to work. Ben looked down at his book. Something scuttled across his desk.

"Mrs Molten!" he gasped. "A cockroach!"

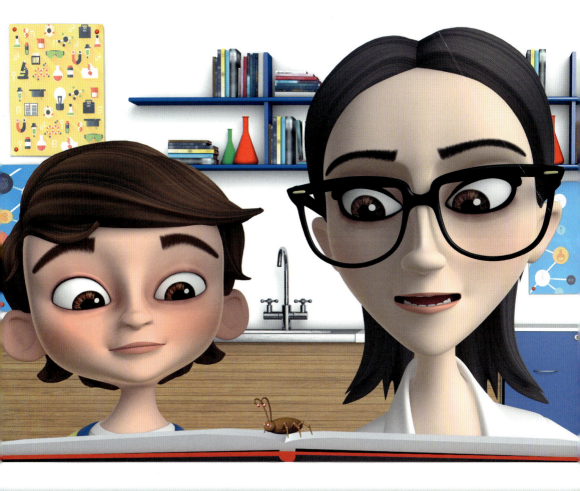

Mrs Molten came over.

"Oh no!" she said with a groan. "We've never had any cockroaches in the school. Today of all days! We'd better get rid of it before the superintendent returns."

Ben reached out to touch the cockroach. "Ow!" he yelped. "It gave me an electric shock!"

The cockroach made a beeping noise.

Mrs Molten peered at it. "This isn't a real insect," she said. "It's a robot!"

There was another beeping noise ... and another. Suddenly, robot cockroaches were pouring out from the cupboard.

They swarmed across the floor and spelled out a message: HERO ACADEMY IS FINISHED!

"Someone must have sent the cockroaches so that we would fail the inspection," said Mrs Molten. "There's only one villain who would have sent in creepy-crawlies like this."

"Who?" Ben asked.

Mrs Molten picked up her tablet.

Doctor Bug

NUMBER 22 MOST WANTED VILLAIN

Catchphrase: Tremble before me, puny humans!

Hobby: going on safari in Wildcroft Woods to spot rare insects.

Likes: pollen squash, honey cake.

Dislikes: magnifying glasses, Venus flytraps.

Beware! This villain may be small but he has armies of robotic insects under his control – so always carry a fly-swatter, just in case!

"Doctor Bug sent the cockroaches!" exclaimed Ben.

"Yes," said Mrs Molten, "and if we don't get rid of them before the superintendent returns, she might shut Hero Academy down!"

Magnus was passing the classroom, carrying a vacuum cleaner. He gasped when he saw all the cockroaches.

"They're robots," explained Mrs Molten.

"Leave it to me," said Magnus. He switched on the vacuum and pointed it at the robotic insects.

Suddenly, the cockroaches started to whir. Their wings unfolded and they rose into the air. Then they flew at Magnus, hitting him like hailstones.

"Ow!" he cried. "Help!"

Ben had an idea. He ran in a circle, faster and faster. Ben made a whirlwind that gathered up all the cockroaches.

"Quick, Magnus!" Ben shouted. "The vacuum!"

Magnus pointed the vacuum cleaner at the cockroach whirlwind. It began to suck the cockroaches inside, faster and faster, until they had all gone.

"What is going on?" said a stern voice. It was the superintendent.

Magnus switched the vacuum cleaner off. "Er ... a cleaning demonstration."

"A what?" snapped the superintendent.

"Yes," said Ben, quickly. "Good heroes always clean up after themselves."

The superintendent looked around. "Well," she said, "I suppose the school is quite clean. Hero Academy has passed the inspection."

The children cheered.

"This time," she added.

Just then, Ben noticed something scuttling up the superintendent's bag. He gasped.

"What's the matter with you?" the superintendent demanded, glaring at Ben.

Behind the superintendent, Mrs Molten put her finger to her lips and shook her head.

"Er … nothing!" Ben spluttered.

Without another word, the superintendent strode off down the corridor.